Searchlight
BOOKS™

What Do You
Know about
Maps?

Using

Political Maps

Rebecca E. Hirsch

Lerner Publications • Minneapolis

Lerner Publications Company
A division of Lerner Publishing Group, Inc.
241 First Avenue North
Minneapolis, MN 55401 USA

For reading levels and more information, look up this title
at www.lernerbooks.com.

Library of Congress Cataloging-in-Publication Data

Names: Hirsch, Rebecca E., author.
Title: Using political maps / Rebecca E. Hirsch.
Description: Minneapolis : Lerner Publications, 2016. | Series: Searchlight books : what
    do you know about maps? | Includes bibliographical references and index.
Identifiers: LCCN 2015036521| ISBN 9781512409475 (lb : alk. paper) | ISBN
    9781512412949 (pb : alk. paper) | ISBN 9781512410747 (eb pdf)
Subjects: LCSH: Map reading—Juvenile literature. | Administrative and political
    divisions—Maps—Juvenile literature.
Classification: LCC GA130 .H56 2016 | DDC 912.01/4—dc23
LC record available at http://lccn.loc.gov/2015036521

Manufactured in the United States of America
1 – VP – 7/15/16

Contents

Chapter 1

WHAT IS A POLITICAL MAP?

Imagine you are trying to find buried treasure. You have a map that leads the way. An *X* on the map marks the spot of the treasure. You don't see an *X* on the ground, of course. But thanks to the map, you know exactly where to dig.

Maps can show us many things about a place. What does this map show?

Maps can serve many purposes. A map may show the location of treasure. It may show natural features on Earth, such as mountains and deserts.

A map may show places that have been created by people. It may show the borders that separate these places. These borders aren't features of the land, the way mountains or deserts are. They are imaginary, like the *X* on the treasure map. A map that shows human places and their borders is called a political map.

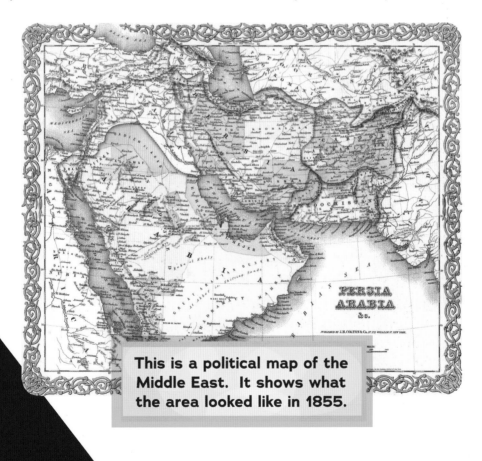

This is a political map of the Middle East. It shows what the area looked like in 1855.

A political map may show different countries and their capitals. It may show states, provinces, counties, cities, and other important places. Any place that was created by people might appear on a political map.

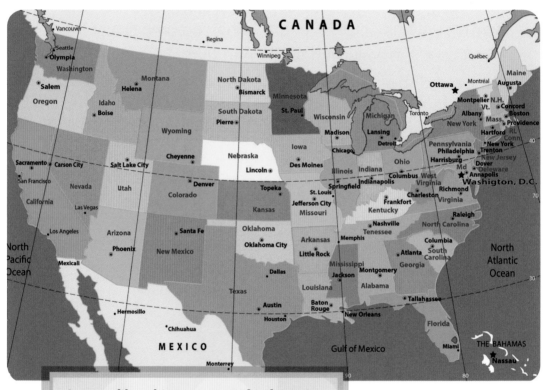

A map like this one may be hanging in your classroom. Maps that show states are political maps.

This political map shows the Great Lakes. They are the blue part of the map near Michigan and other northern states. But it does not show smaller lakes within these states.

No single map can show everything. For this reason, cartographers (people who make maps) choose what places they want to emphasize. They include only the features that will be important to people using the map.

A political map may show important bodies of water, such as rivers and lakes. But you probably will not see mountains or deserts on a political map. You'll mostly just see human-made things.

Globes vs. Political Maps

If you wanted to see all the countries on Earth, you could look at a globe. A globe is a tiny model of Earth. It shows the true shape of Earth—a sphere. A globe can show you all the countries on the planet, but it can show you only part of Earth at one time. If you want to see countries on the other side of the world, you have to turn the globe.

GLOBES SHOW ALL SEVEN CONTINENTS, BUT YOU MUST TURN THE GLOBE TO SEE THEM.

Maps through History

People have been making maps for thousands of years. In ancient times, they painted or carved maps of their surroundings on rock or clay. As civilization grew, mapmakers drew maps of distant lands based on reports and drawings from explorers and travelers. Modern cartographers rely on aerial and satellite photography to map the world. They draw maps by putting together these photographs like puzzle pieces.

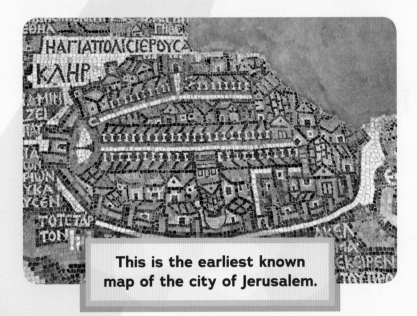

This is the earliest known map of the city of Jerusalem.

If you want to see all the countries of the world at once, you will have to look at a political map. A political map of the entire Earth shows all the countries of the world. A political map may show the entire Earth or any part of Earth. It may show many countries or just one country. Or it may show just one state, such as the state where you live.

Political maps of the world show all the continents on a single page.

Chapter 2

WHAT'S ON A POLITICAL MAP?

Political maps use a special
language. It includes symbols,
names, numbers, lines, and colors.
You can learn how to read this language.
Political maps use
symbols that are simple
and easy to understand.
The meaning of these
symbols is shown in a legend,
or key. The legend is usually in a
box near a corner of the map.

The box in the right-hand corner of this map
helps you understand the symbols on the map.
What is this guide to the map's symbols called?

Dots and Stars

Dots on a political map often stand for cities and towns. Sometimes the dots are the same size. Sometimes they are different sizes. Look at the legend to understand the meaning of different-sized dots. Large dots may show large cities with lots of people. Small dots may show smaller cities and towns.

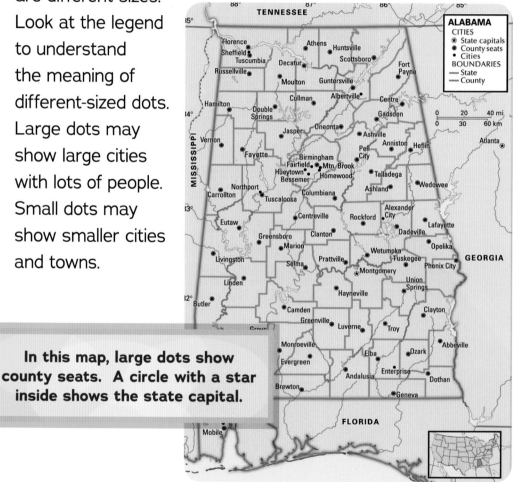

In this map, large dots show county seats. A circle with a star inside shows the state capital.

Learn More about Political Maps

Books

Hirsch, Rebecca E. *What's Great about Washington, DC?* Minneapolis: Lerner Publications, 2015. Take a fun-filled tour of the United States' capital, complete with maps and interesting facts.

Isaacs, Sally Senzell. *Ultimate Globetrotting World Atlas.* Washington, DC: National Geographic Society, 2014. Learn fascinating information about the countries of the world with fun facts, political maps, and games.

Rajczak, Kristen. *Latitude and Longitude.* New York: Gareth Stevens, 2015. Check out this book to learn more about latitude and longitude.

Websites

Enchanted Learning: World Geography
http://www.enchantedlearning.com/geography
Check out this collection of maps, printouts, flags, and more from Enchanted Learning.

50 States
http://www.50states.com
This site has fun facts about the fifty states and plenty of maps you can print.

Math Is Fun: Coloring—the Four Color Theorem
http://www.mathsisfun.com/activity/coloring.html
Investigate the four-color theorem with coloring activities and puzzles at the Math Is Fun website.

Index

Photo Acknowledgments

The images in this book are used with the permission of: © iStockphoto.com/VladSt, p. 4; G. W. Colton/Wikimedia Commons, p. 5; © Sasa1867/Deposit Photos, pp. 6, 7; © iStockphoto.com/ Christopher Futcher, pp. 8, 30; © iStockphoto.com/WitR, p. 9; © Dorling Kindersley/Getty Images, p. 10; © Encyclopaedia Britannica/Universal Images Group Limited/Alamy, pp. 11, 12; © iStockphoto. com/omersukrugoksu, p. 13; © iStockphoto.com/FrankRamspott, p. 14; © Lonely Planet/Getty Images, p. 15; © MAPS.com/Corbis, p. 16; © Volina/Deposit Photos, p. 17; © iStockphoto.com/Zmiy, p. 18; © Mike Kowalski/Illustration Works/Getty Images, p. 19; © JRTBurr/Deposit Photos, pp. 20, 22; © Historic Map Works LLC/Getty Images, pp. 21, 26; © iStockphoto.com/PeterHermesFurian, p. 23; © Laura Westlund/Independent Picture Service, pp. 24, 25, 34, 35; © Steve Vidler/SuperStock, p. 27; © iStockphoto.com/stevegeer, p. 28 (left); © iStockphoto.com/hapiphoto, p. 28; © Blend Images/ SuperStock, p. 29; © iStockphoto.com/ilynx_v, p. 31; Library of Congress Geography and Map Division, p. 32; © olinchuk/Deposit Photos, p. 33; © iStockphoto.com/STEEX, p. 36.

Front cover: © Laura Westlund/Independent Picture Service.

Main body text set in Adrianna Regular 14/20
Typeface provided by Chank